Modern Software Engineering

A survey of principles and practices for individuals, teams, and organisations.

Dean Michael Berris Copyright 2024.

Copyright

Copyright 2024 Dean Michael Berris.

All copies of this book are licensed under the Creative Commons Attribution NonCommercial ShareAlike 4.0 International License. See https://creativecommons.org/licenses/by-nc-sa/4.0/ for details.

Foreword

Dear reader,

First, I would like to thank you for purchasing a copy of this book from my website at www.deanberris.com — if this copy was forwarded to you, consider buying a copy for yourself as well if you like it.

This is a collection of previously published articles on medium.com and edited to include additional questions that you can ask about your current software engineering practices. These questions are designed to help you see where you currently are and how far you can take your organisation.

I also offer personal coaching, team coaching, and engineering practice development for organisations looking to modernise their software engineering practices.

You can find out more through my website at www.deanberris.com.

Thank you for reading!

- Dean

Dedication

This book is dedicated to my partner Jeni, who has supported me throughout the years and has stuck with me through the thick and thin of life.

This book is also for my children Julia and Zachary. I hope they find this as an example of how, in our own ways, we can contribute to the world. I also hope they learn that hard work and continuous learning leads to a fruitful life.

Copyright

Foreword

Dedication

Introduction

Chapter 1: System Design

    The Importance of Systems Design

    Components of System Design

    Principles of System Design

    Modern Design Patterns

    Conclusion

    Questions

Chapter 2: Testing

    Learning the hard way

    Testing Levels

    Test-Driven Development

    Automated Testing

    Modern Testing Techniques

    Conclusion

    Questions

Chapter 3: Documentation

    Filling the gap

    Types of Documentation

    Why write documentation?

    What does effective documentation look like?

    Documentation in Open Source Projects

Conclusion

  Questions

Chapter 4: Deployment

  One step at a time

  Deployment Models

  Deployment Strategies

  Tooling

  Conclusion

  Questions

Chapter 5: Continuous Evolution

  Cautionary Tale

  Agile and DevOps

  Continuous Integration, Delivery, and Deployment

  Version Control Systems

  Monitoring and Observability

  Conclusion

  Questions

Epilogue

Introduction

Software Engineering has a short but rich history dating back from the early development of programmable computers. Ever since computers supported stored programs in digital form, a whole practice around making software manageable to produce, execute, and change became as important as the computers themselves.

Software Engineering is a quintessential human endeavour which is becoming more mature the longer we do it. Even in the age of Artificial Intelligence systems being able to aid in the development of software, based on my personal experience with some cutting edge technologies in this field, the human judgment is still an essential part of the process. Unless that changes, I believe Software Engineering is still a valuable endeavour to pursue which will evolve to require more of the human judgment—but the mechanical parts might just get quicker.

I decided to write the series originally to share the knowledge and observations I've gained in the past 20 years with some anecdotes in the introductions. I've preserved these stories and anecdotes because I believe those narrative elements make the series more human and relatable even in this compilation.

Each chapter is an article in the series, preserved as much as possible with some editorial changes. Some have been modified to have more headings and exposition. All the articles have been augmented with a section on questions to ask and thoughts to ponder, so that you can use this for self reflection or conversations within your team.

Chapter 1: System Design

"Make it simple, but significant." - Don Draper, Mad Men

Growing up in the late '80s and early '90s, my exposure to computers was limited to almost exclusively gaming consoles (I considered the Atari 800 and Commodore 64 gaming computers because I only ever saw games being run on them) or the early x86 systems. It wasn't until I got to university in the 2000s that I got a hold of a Sun Microsystems SPARC workstation, UNIX, and Slackware Linux that I could install on my Intel 486 machine at home.

Back then, software development was mostly about software that ran locally on your machine or, if you had access to it, a shared time computer with significantly more processing power available to you to… do business-relevant things. At university, I remember hearing about a program used by computer scientists that needed a multicore processor to generate thousands of students' schedules; it took weeks to generate and print the schedules. Up to this day, I'm still not sure which took longer — the running of the program or the printing to paper.

Today, the majority of software being developed either runs on the cloud, runs on a device that requires access to the cloud, or powers other software that also runs on the cloud. It's very rare to be working on a software system that works in confined spaces (e.g., embedded software systems) that do not have access to a more powerful computing platform elsewhere. Accounting systems now crunch heaps of data hosted in server farms either on a company's premises or out in a data warehouse. Sales systems now have customer relationships managed by a third party with plugins developed by yet more third-party or in-house developers.

But how do these software systems get built today to serve hundreds to millions of users while still maintaining the performance and responsiveness we've grown to expect from the software we use today?

As a software engineer for the better part of 20 years, I've seen many systems being developed from every level of the stack. Interrupt handlers in the DOS days to JavaScript-driven animation and even no-code report generation. A couple of weeks ago, I even got ChatGPT-4 to generate some Python code based on some descriptions I gave it for what I wanted! But that's a story for another day.

In this chapter, I'm writing about systems design, how it's become a critical part of the modern software engineering practice, and how it will be one of the key areas where human software engineers can still deliver value in the short and medium term.

The Importance of Systems Design

Once upon a time, I was a software engineer in a company that had issues handling the load of the success they'd brought upon themselves. I'll call this company Friendster. When I joined the company, the project I was put on was already late and had many bugs related to memory management. Their core service (yes, it was a microservice before we called it that back in 2007) was written in C++ but had memory leaks, took too long to handle requests, and was designed to cache and serve data in memory. It needed to be stateless but ended up becoming stateful.

A few weeks into the project, I pleaded with senior engineering leadership to ditch the iteration of this service and instead write something from-scratch that met the requirements; it would be a drop-in replacement of the existing implementation. We had a deadline to beat because the service could only handle another few months of growth before it could no longer handle the size of the cache the way it rehydrated it.

Restarting the service took longer than the time it could stay up until the memory leaks took it down. This was a "bet my career" moment, but I barely had one. We had to make it work.

In comes system design. The first thing we did was list out what requirements the system had to meet, what the contracts were between the dependent services (PHP frontend code) and this core service, and a plan on how we were going to meet three key non-technical requirements: performance, efficiency, and resilience.

System design involves understanding the constraints under which the system must perform its function, what the required functions are, and what properties of the system are important to keep relative to all other properties. Once you have these defined, you can start designing a system that meets the requirements and systematically plan out the solution's delivery.

Components of System Design

When we talk about system design, there are usually several components that this entails:

- **Architecture** — what does the overall solution look like? Does it involve multiple subsystems? Are there individual components that make up a whole? How do they interact, and how do they relate to one another?

- **Topology** — Is there a layering to the solution? If this is a distributed system, where are the component services located physically or logically in relation to one another?

- **Low-level design** — What interfaces do you have defined through which different parts of the systems interact? Are there specific algorithms you're using to address key aspects of the solution (performance, efficiency, throughput, resilience, etc.)?

It helps to understand first things like: is the system self-contained (i.e., will have no access to external resources), or is it distributed? Will it have a user interface, or will it be non-interactive (e.g., does it generate a report that's printed out, or will it require human or another system's inputs during its operation)? Does it need to handle a lot of traffic? Is it meant to only be used by ten people at any given time, or will 10 million users use it at any given time?

Once you have answers to some of these questions, making decisions through system design principles will be easier.

Principles of System Design

Several key principles to designing software systems in this modern age didn't quite come up until systems needed to scale — from being a single-user system to one that should be able to handle thousands and even millions of users at a time. Here are some we'll cover in this chapter:

- Scalability

- Reliability

- Maintainability

- Availability

- Security

Scalability

A system is scalable when it can be deployed to handle the growth in load with proportional growth in resources. The scaling factor of a system is defined as the growth in the amount of resources required to serve the growth in load on the system. We encounter two typical scaling cases with software systems: vertical scaling and horizontal scaling.

Vertical scaling refers to providing more headroom or single-machine resources to the software system to handle a growth in requirements. Consider the case of a network-attached storage appliance. The more storage you provide through the appliance, the more data it can store. If you need it to handle more concurrent connections and I/O Operations (IOPs), you'd typically need to add more compute power and network interfaces to handle the increased load.

Horizontal scaling refers to replicating a system or multiple machines with copies of the software to handle growth in requirements. Consider the case of a static web content server hidden behind a load balancer. Adding more servers allows more clients to connect and download the content from the web servers, and when the load has subsided, the number of web servers can be scaled down to the right size for current demand.

Some systems can handle hybrid or diagonal scaling. For example, some distributed database architectures allow for splitting the compute and storage nodes so that compute-heavy workloads can use the nodes with more compute resources. In contrast, the IOPs' heavy workloads can run on the storage+compute nodes. Stream processing applications, for example, might separate workloads that require more memory and compute (e.g., event sourcing or analytics workloads) and scale those appropriately and independently from the IOPs' heavy workloads (e.g., compression and archiving).

Reliability

A system is reliable when it can tolerate partial failure and recovery without severely degrading the quality of service. Part of a system's reliability includes the predictability of its operations in terms of latency, throughput, and adherence to an agreed-upon range of operations.

Usual approaches to ensuring system reliability involve the following:

- Setting up system redundancies to support transparent or minimal-disruption failover.

- Building in fault tolerance in the case of internal errors or input-induced failures.

- Clearly defining contracts and targets for latency, throughput, and availability.

- Setting up sufficient standby capacity to meet burst and organic growth in load.

- Service quality safeguards to enforce rate limits and customer/operation isolation.

- Implementing graceful service degradation in overload or catastrophic failure scenarios.

The key thing to remember for making reliable systems is to handle potential failures in a well-defined manner that dependent systems can react to. This means if there are inputs that could cause the system to be available for everyone, then it's not a reliable system. Likewise, if the system depends on another system that could be unreliable, then it should handle the unreliability with strategies to ensure reliability.

Maintainability

A system is maintainable when changed with commensurate effort and deployed with minimal user disruption. This requires implementing the system in a manner that assumes requirements will change and that it is flexible enough to handle the foreseeable changes in direction. It also means ensuring that the code is readable so that the next set of maintainers (which could be the same team but looking at it with new eyes in the future) can maintain the software and evolve it to meet future needs.

Nobody wants to be stuck maintaining software that is rigid, hard to change, not well organised, poorly documented, poorly designed, untested, and haphazardly put together.

Ensuring the code quality is high is part of engineering excellence reflecting professionalism and excellent craftsmanship. Not only is it a good thing to do, but it's known to allow high-functioning and high-performance engineering teams to deliver software that can be changed and extended to deliver value consistently.

Availability

If your service is not available, it may not exist.

Systems design should address how a system should stay available to remain relevant to customers and users of the system. This means:

- Introduce redundancies to handle underlying system failures.

- Having backup and restore scenarios and operational guides to bringing a system back up from hard failures.

- Remove as many single points of failures from the system.

- Along with horizontal scalability, have regional replicas and set up content delivery networks (where appropriate) to make your data available.

- Monitor your system's availability from your customers' perspective to better understand how your system is serving customers.

I learned early in my career that a flaky and unavailable system can sometimes be the biggest cause of losing your customers' trust. Once you lose your customers' trust, it will be very hard to regain it.

Security

System design should address security as a key aspect, especially in the age of internet-connected systems, where security threats and vulnerabilities can cause actual harm to our customers and the users of the systems. The goal of building secure software isn't to achieve perfection but rather to understand the risks involved in breaches and attacks. Having a proper security threat model and a systematic approach to understanding where the risks lie and what kinds of threats are worth prioritising and designing mitigations for is the start of a secure design and engineering practice.

Security is no longer optional today as our software systems become part of mission-critical services to more parts of modern society. Taking security seriously in the systems we design from the beginning takes us closer to being able to rely better on software that we build and deploy to meet our users' needs. Earning our customers' trust is hard enough, and it only takes one breach to lose a good part of it.

Modern Design Patterns

Given the above aspects, some patterns for modern distributed systems have come up that address a number of these aspects in different ways. Let's explore some of the more popular design patterns we see today regarding the five aspects of system design.

Microservices

With the rise of distributed systems which focus on building reliability and scale through redundancy, efficiency, and performance through horizontal scaling, and resilience through decoupling parts of the system as independently operating services, the term "microservices" has gained popularity by achieving the following:

- Tying independent services' development, deployment, operation, and maintenance to teams that own these services within a larger business operation. We can do this either by serving external customers directly or indirectly via internal customers through an API.

- Allowing the microservice to scale independently according to demand.

- Providing service through a well-defined contract allows the implementation to evolve to stay as a self-contained service or a system of services.

Looking through our aspects, microservices have attractive properties, which makes it a good pattern to follow if it applies to the use case:

- **Scalability**: Stateless microservices are typically designed to be horizontally scalable and can also benefit from vertical scaling. In the case of microservices deployed within a containerised orchestration environment (e.g., Kubernetes clusters), the microservices can even run on the same nodes yielding better utilisation of existing hardware and scaling to demand with available capacity. One downside is the deployment complexity as a microservice grows in scale and criticality in a graph of microservices.

- **Reliability**: Stateless microservices are typically hosted behind a load balancer and geographically distributed to avoid regional outages taking all the system's capacity. One downside of building reliability with stateless microservices is that the storage system will typically need to be as reliable as or more reliable than the microservice's implementation/deployment. Stateful microservices then suffer from the worst of both approaches, where the cost of reliability is typically in the form of over-provisioning to handle potential outages.

- **Maintainability**: Microservices that implement a well-defined and stable contract served through an API allow clients to program against that API and the implementation to evolve independently. However, coordinating changes to an API involves potentially costly client migrations and cross-team coordination, introducing a period of the microservice having multiple actively supported versions until the last clients migrate from the older implementation. This only gets worse as more clients start interacting with a microservice.

- **Availability**: Microservices typically rely on the deployment environment and external infrastructure to meet the availability requirements of clients. The downside of this is the reliance on the particular infrastructure on which a microservice is deployed to provide the high-availability solution. Systems like service meshes and software load balancers become critical pieces of infrastructure that are no longer controlled by the implementation. This could be a good thing but can also be a constant source of maintenance as these systems also have update cycles and operational costs.

- **Security**: Authentication, Authorisation, Identity Management, and Credential Management can be delegated to middleware or through external mechanisms (e.g., workload identities in Kubernetes), where the microservice implementation can focus on integrating the relevant business logic. The downside, as in availability, is that these external pieces of the solution become critical pieces of infrastructure that bring their own operational costs on top of the microservice implementation.

Microservices are a great way to break up a large application where logical partitions requiring their own scaling and reliability domains can be identified. When starting from scratch, though, it's less ideal to design microservices from the beginning because of the risk of breaking down the services into too small pieces. The cost of communication between microservices — typically as HTTP or gRPC requests — is significant and should only be incurred if necessary. A good way of determining whether functionality fits within a service is by following a practice like Domain Driven Design or Functional Decomposition.

Serverless

As in microservices-based solutions, using serverless implementations further delegates key pieces of the functionality of serving requests to the underlying infrastructure. If, in Microservices, the service is served by a persistent process, Serverless solutions typically implement only an entry point to handle a request to an endpoint (typically a URI via HTTP or gRPC). In Serverless deployments, no actual servers are being configured, but rather the deployment environment spins up resources as necessary to handle requests as they come in. Sometimes, those resources stay up for some time to amortise the cost of bringing them up, but that's meant to be an implementation detail.

Let's look through the aspects of system design to see how Serverless solutions stack up:

- **Scalability**: Serverless solutions are as horizontally scalable as microservices, if not more so because they are designed to be right-sized on demand. The downside of this approach is the need for more control and complete delegation of the scaling functionality to the underlying Serverless infrastructure.

- **Reliability**: Serverless reliability depends on the capacity for horizontal scaling and network traffic routing. This has the same downsides as the Microservices solution.

- **Maintainability**: Serverless implementations are more maintainable than microservices due to the focus on the business logic for handling requests with minimal boilerplate. This has the same issues with API evolution that microservices have.

- **Availability**: Serverless deployments are as available as the environment they're deployed in. This has the same issues, with the underlying infrastructure becoming more critical than the solution itself.

- **Security**: Serverless implementations completely depend on the underlying infrastructure's security configuration. This has the same issues, with the underlying infrastructure becoming more critical than the actual solution itself.

Serverless solutions, or Functions as a Service, are a very attractive way of prototyping and even deploying production-grade solutions by focusing on the business logic and value and letting the underlying infrastructure handle the service's scalability, reliability, and availability. It's a typical starting point for getting a solution with minimal operational burden up and running, and for most prototypes, it's a great way to prove our hypothesis.

It's also a typical experience that once these solutions hit the scaling limits, the costs associated with running these become high enough. These are turned into more optimal microservice implementations tuned to the scale needed.

Event-Driven

There are some problem domains where online transaction processing is not required, and microservices and serverless implementations don't quite fit the bill. Consider the cases where processing transactions can be done in the background or as resources are available. Another case is for background processing activities where the outcomes are not necessarily interactive.

Event-driven systems follow the pattern of having an event source, and event sinks where events (messages) come from and are sent, respectively. Processing happens from subscribers and publishers to these sources and sinks, respectively. An example of an event-driven system is a chatbot that can participate in many conversations (event sources and sinks) and handle messages as they come in.

Distributed event-driven systems can have multiple concurrent message handlers waiting on the same sources, potentially publishing too many sinks that act as sources for other message handlers. This pattern of chaining together processors through sinks and sources is called an event pipeline. Typically, there's a single implementation of the sinks and sources that provides a message queue interface and scales according to the demand for messages coming through the system. Many distributed queue management systems can also benefit from diagonal scaling effectively, like Apache Kafka, RabbitMQ, etc.

Let's examine distributed event-driven systems through our five aspects:

- **Scalability**: Both the message/event broker implementation and the message handlers can scale independently. Some downsides come up when too many messages/events are being handled, and the demand on the event broker grows far beyond the capacity available in the system.

- **Reliability**: Good message broker implementations provide high levels of reliability, and it's a good idea to not create your own message broker implementation. The downside is the dependency on a solution that meets the reliability needs of the solution (e.g., handling financial transactions is very different from handling instant messaging routing in chat rooms).

- **Maintainability**: If you use a flexible message interchange format like Protocol Buffers, it's plausible to evolve the writers and readers of messages while using the same data description language. This still requires coordination, but not as onerous as evolving API contracts across live transaction processing systems (as in microservices and serverless implementations).

- **Availability**: Since messages are typically stored in durable media, event-driven systems are usually easier to make available, especially since they're typically non-interactive applications. The availability cost may come from stale messages and unbounded queue processing delays.
- **Security**: Event-driven systems must manage data availability independently of identity and credentials. Ensuring that only certain services or message processors can access specific message queues or logs becomes a full-time job as more varied data gets plumbed through the system.

Conclusion

Modern software engineering entails designing scalable, reliable, maintainable, available, and secure systems. Designing distributed systems requires substantial rigour as the realities of modern system complexity grow with society's demands for better software services. We reviewed three modern design patterns for distributed systems and worked through the five aspects of well-designed systems.

As software engineers, we are responsible for designing systems that address the key concerns of distributed systems in the modern age.

Questions

Use the following to reflect on your software engineering practices related to systems design:

- When was the last time you evaluated your system's design? Is it still meeting the current requirements?
- Pick a system or a part of a system you've been working on and use the aspects identified in the chapter (Scalability, Reliability,

Maintainability, Availability, Security). Do you see any deficiencies in the current design? Are there changes you can make to address those deficiencies?

- When working in a team, which of the aspects do you focus on when reviewing designs?

- Does your organisation have a consistent process for reviewing system designs before, during, and after the development of the software?

- Do you have opportunities to learn about new practices in software engineering or testing your system design knowledge? Do you have a consistent practice for keeping up to speed on developments in the industry and augmenting your current knowledge and skills?

- Do you have mentors or peers that have experience or expertise in this field that you can learn from? Are there resources they can recommend that you can consume?

- How much time do you devote to learning about systems design on your own or in your organisation? Are you spending so much time trying to keep up with the system or in constantly remaking solutions that don't seem to meet the requirements?

Chapter 2: Testing

"If debugging is the process of removing software bugs, then programming must be the act of putting them in." – Edsger Djikstra

Writing automated software tests is like playing a game of telephone with yourself – you're the only person you can blame when you misunderstand what the message is. It's hard enough if you're writing tests for your own code, but consider the case when you're writing tests for code that someone else has written that wasn't being tested in the first place. Now it's like trying to understand what the message was from a piece of paper that's been washed in blue jean pockets… three times!

That's for tests that are written after the code being tested has already been written.

Now consider the practice of writing the tests first – it's like playing mastermind with yourself, by first writing some plausible-looking specification or test the ensure that the solution you will write is going to "do the right thing". But if you took computer science, then that sounds very much like solving the halting problem – only worse because now you need to prove not just to yourself but to the compiler/interpreter that the thing you want it to do is the right thing.

So why has testing been such an integral part of the modern software engineering practice for the last 20 years – whether it's test-first or test-last, we professional software engineers still need to think about how the software is tested and verified to meet the requirements?

Learning the hard way

It's story time again.

In Chapter 1, I wrote about how I learned the hard way how to design systems to suit modern scaling, reliability, availability, maintainability, and security requirements. Designing a solution only goes so far, because at the end of the day, the solution needs to be implemented – sometimes, it has to be done by one or more teams of people.

You can imagine that the coordination of efforts across teams is going to be a major source of issues, but is there something we can do to reduce this burden?

In comes automated testing – especially the kind that specifies behaviour instead of tests the implementation.

While I was at Friendster, I had the luxury of knowing what exactly the client of the service I was working on expected. However, it wasn't fully specified – we had a protocol we were following (this was before Protocol Buffers were popular) and some URIs that were being called by these clients. The semantics weren't fully spelled out, but we had a captive audience – I can read the client code and figure out what the expectations are from the current implementation.

This was important – instead of creating a brand new protocol or creating a new contract, we started from known requirements that we can write as automated tests. One of the first few things I had to do was turn these tests into specifications I can program against, and incrementally bring the implementation to a point where it fulfilled the requirements.

There were two products out of that effort:

- The C++ Network Library – a reasonably performant C++ implementation of an HTTP client and server, upon which the service I was rewriting would be using.

- The memcache++ library – a reasonably performant C++ implementation of the memcache protocol, with support for sharding and virtual node pools.

Both of these open source solutions were the outcomes of internally defined technical requirements.

We started from an existing system, broke it down into component parts, and then implemented the solutions incrementally to a point where we can share the non-business-critical parts as open source software.

You might ask then, why did I need to start from the tests?

Because the tests allowed me to fill in the solution to meet the requirements in an incremental and predictable manner. Having the tests there allowed me and folks reviewing the code I was writing to understand what the requirements were and verify them automatically by running the tests. This allowed us to gain the confidence we needed incrementally that we were getting a solution that met our needs.

Having the tests there allowed me to focus on what was necessary and sufficient to provide the functionality, while giving me the confidence to refactor and improve the solution and quickly verify whether I've broken tests that encode the requirements. I've been able to catch so many bugs and deliver features so quickly by having the tests encompass the requirements to be fearlessly refactoring along the way.

This was around 2007–2008 when a lot of these concepts (like Test-Driven-Development and Behaviour-Driven-Development) were just becoming popular, but usually in the enterprise software industry. Here I was taking some of those good ideas and applying them to micro services and horizontally scalable systems!

Fast forward a few years, we're now at 2023 and testing has become somewhat of a dirty word in some circles (TDD, and BDD tend to burn a lot of people mostly due to misunderstandings of the tenets) and has become an afterthought that we're asking coding AIs to make unit tests for code we write. This is a bit of a shame because the freedom that high-performing software engineering teams that employ the right kinds of tests have to adapt to changing requirements and improve the implementation of solutions is so valuable, teams that don't invest in it early enough tend to realise too late that testing would have saved them major outages, sleepless nights due to bugs creeping into production, or just lost business due to poor solution quality and low velocity.

In this chapter, cover the role of testing in modern software engineering, and how doing it right sets you and your team up for success in the industry.

Testing Levels

Before we go further, it would be good to understand the different levels or categories of tests. If you've never written tests before, it might be good to know that there's quite a robust taxonomy of testing terms so that you can at least follow along with the discussions happening around them.

- **User Acceptance Testing** – typically automated tests which ensure that a software system fits an end-users requirements. Simulating end users typically involves driving the software's user interface (browser-based automated tests for Web UIs, application drivers for native application UIs, API service clients, etc.) to perform what a user would do, and observing the outcomes of those actions to see whether it meets the acceptance criteria for the software. This is typically the highest level of testing covering as much of the software system as a whole.

- **System Testing** – typically automated tests that test the functional and non-functional properties of a system. Here, a system could be a fully integrated application or a subsystem with associated components. System tests are typically more comprehensive than User Acceptance Tests (UATs).

- **Integration Testing** – typically automated tests that test the interaction of multiple components working as a subsystem in an integration environment (typically a testing harness or application scaffold) which facilitates the wiring and testing of the integrated components. Integration tests typically exercise logical subsystems of a full solution that work together to provide a specific set of functions.

- **Unit Testing** – typically automated tests that tests the functionality of a single component (not necessarily a single class) in isolation. Dependencies may be substituted by functionally equivalent implementations to facilitate the simulation of these dependencies in a controlled (and sometimes, contrived) manner.

In some cases, you may come across the need to have manual or human-driven tests to cover some unpredictable or combinatorially huge spaces of possibilities (consider computer games, AI models, control systems, etc.). Those still have a good place in the software engineering industry, but in this chapter, I'll focus on automated testing cases.

Now that we have some definitions in place, let's dive into some modern software engineering approaches to testing and how it's changing the way we solve problems.

Test-Driven Development

Test Driven Development or TDD is a methodology for implementing software by writing the tests (or specifications) first as executable code, seeing the test fail (red first), implementing a solution to satisfy the requirements, seeing the test succeed (go green), refactoring the solution for readability and flexibility while keeping the tests running successfully (stay green), and iterating. Here's a bit more explanation for each of the steps in this methodology:

1. **Write a failing test to represent a requirement.** This might use a class that doesn't exist yet, or a method that isn't implemented yet, or a case that isn't handled by an existing implementation yet, or some new behaviour that the system doesn't perform yet – whatever the new requirement is, write a test that represents that requirement as something executable and that initially fails. This step lets us think about the missing functionality and how it's intended to be used at any level – the test could be a UAT, System Test, Integration Test, or Unit Test.

2. **Implement the solution to meet the requirement (go green).** The initial implementation to meet the requirement may be the simplest thing that works, or a simple "return the thing

the test expects" (I know, this feels like cheating, but trust the process...) just so that you can see the test "go green". This step forces us to think about the most direct way to solve the problem so that we can get to the next step and re-do this cycle.

3. **Refactor ruthlessly while keeping the tests green (stay green).** Do not pass step 2 here, because the meat of the software engineering happens in this step, where we get to look at the interfaces used in the tests and in the implementation to see whether we're getting closer to a more maintainable and flexible solution or whether we need more tests to find the patterns. The more tests you have covering the functionality of the system, the more you need to refactor not just the implementation but the tests – if you're also following domain driven design, this lets you refine the models you have in the system so you evolve your understanding of the solution along with the changes to the model.

4. **Iterate.** As you cover more and more of the functional and non-functional requirements of the system at different levels (UATs, System Tests, Integration Tests, Unit Tests), you'll inevitably find that some requirements are no longer requirements, that existing ones have changed slightly due to new business requirements, and that you probably have to start over with some subsystem. Recognizing when to go adding more tests, removing tests, optimizing performance or efficiency, or just calling it done and moving on is an important part of the whole process. As long as you're not done, go back to step 1.

Note that you can start following TDD even if you've already got a code base that doesn't have tests. You can start from the top down (UATs down to unit tests) or bottom up (unit tests to UATs) and along the way start refactoring your interfaces to the ones you'd feel more confident represents the logical components or your domain models better.

Following TDD from the start has a number of advantages:

- **You are forced to think of the requirements and the design while you're writing the tests.** Code that's hard to test usually means it's not following good design practices. If you're finding that you're not able to express the test well means that you don't understand the requirement as well, which forces you to first understand what the requirements are before you write the tests.

- **You have more confidence that the solution you have is meeting the requirements even before it reaches production.** Catching the issues ahead of time saves you from the foreseeable headaches from production. It also allows you to focus on the problem solving with the guide already there rather than waiting too long to know whether you've met the requirement when it's live. Instead of spending your time debugging, you're spending your time solving other problems and delivering value incrementally with confidence.

- **You have time to tidy up and make it nice.** TDD explicitly builds in the time for refactoring as part of the development process – not something that's deferred for later. If you're in a time crunch and need to defer refactoring, then it's something that can be picked up later too with the confidence that your tests represent the state of the requirements and that the implementation quality can be improved as part of the process.

That's all nice as well, but there's a cost to TDD that we need to acknowledge too and some downsides.

- **Writing and running automated tests isn't cheap.** Some kinds of tests are harder to write than others, and they're not all yielding the same value either. Writing UATs may require specialised knowledge of specific testing frameworks, or access to special hardware that's not readily available (powerful GPUs or FPGAs for example) when simulating production deployments. Some require full deployments of multiple services, and standing those up for the purpose of testing might not be cost-effective so some corners may be cut.

- **It's hard to show value of test code especially when it's seen as an opportunity cost.** A lot of people still think that tests are a waste of time because what matters is shipping stuff that works – and that if they fail in production we'll just hack around it because we need to make enough money so the funding doesn't run out. Unfortunately, substituting shipping code to production in lieu of tests means you're risking the effectiveness of your solution and your business every time you deploy code and new functionality. Even though TDD is a nice practice to follow and there are heaps of success stories showing why following TDD is a good idea, unless effective test coverage is seen as an insurance policy for future outages and requirements changes, then it's going to be a hard sell.

- **When you conflate effective testing with 100% test coverage, you will have a bad time.** TDD isn't about getting to 100% test coverage, but rather it focuses on representing requirements as executable tests. You can have as many tests as you like as long as they represent what's important to the system you're building. Having 100% test coverage isn't a representation of how effective your tests are in representing what's important to the solution. It could be that a smaller set of tests gets you the best value in ensuring that the problem you're setting out to solve is being solved.

TDD isn't the panacea to all software quality issues we're encountering in the world. It is however a practice that can help keep what's important in focus so that we can engineer systems that meet the requirements with confidence.

Automated Testing

If you already follow TDD, that's great. But if you don't, it's still important that you have tests that you can run automatically in the following scenarios:

- **At development time, in the "inner developer loop".** If you cannot run tests in your integrated development environment or your workstation to quickly verify that your solutions are doing what they're supposed to be doing then you'll have a bad time.

Ensuring that automated tests are quick to build/run and that they're representative of the important requirements is a significant productivity booster that's worth investing in. If there's nothing else you do but write automated tests that developers can run on their workstations, you'll already reach 80% of the benefits of automated testing.

- **Maintain a regression testing suite.** Whenever bugs are filed or discovered, the first thing that should be done is to reproduce it with a failing test. This way you can manage the bug fixing process as if it's another requirement expressed as a test that catches regressions (this means, that the software doesn't exhibit a bug that's already been fixed in the past). The more bugs you turn into regression tests, the better you can express the actual requirements on the system more extensively and prevent them from recurring in the future.

- **Test non-functional aspects of the system too.** Non-functional requirements refer to qualities of the system that aren't strictly tied to functionality – things like throughput, latency, resource consumption, minimum load requirements, amongst other observable properties. Automating these lets you make them part of the design and implementation requirements so that they're always taken into consideration when changes are being made to the system.

Automated testing is becoming a key tool for delivering competitive and higher-quality software systems, especially in the modern software engineering practices we see today. Given the complexity and criticality of the systems we're building and deploying, it's hard to see how we can manage this without automated testing moving forward.

Modern Testing Techniques

Let's say you've implemented the automated tests, you have UATs, System Tests, Integration Tests, and Unit Tests that you can run. You also have a regression test suite and non-functional requirements expressed as automated tests. How can you bring your testing practices to the modern software engineering era?

Especially for software that's developed and deployed as distributed systems in the cloud orchestrated in an environment like Kubernetes where the control plane manages the placement and management of workloads and resources respectively, and public cloud providers providing managed resources for network presence and geographical diversity, the application architectures are getting more and more complex. Testing these applications becomes very hard and expensive.

Here are a few things to consider to manage this complexity and ensure that you can keep up with the demands on modern large-scale globally available services:

- **Invest in continuous integration and continuous delivery.** Testing before your software hits production only gets you as far as your testing goes, but the realities of production are rarely anticipated in development. Having a way of continuously shipping code that's tested in an integration environment into production in a controlled and safe manner is key to being able to adapt your solution to the realities of production. Because you've already invested in tests, bugs you find in production can then be expressed as failing tests and automatically run through your continuous integration (CI) and continuous deployment (CD) pipelines. This reduces time-to-market and shortens the feedback cycle for engineering teams.

- **Invest in fuzzing and automated fault finding.** There are heaps of solutions for automatically injecting faults in systems you depend on whether they be remote API services or internal components. Fuzzing is an approach to testing which uses randomly generated inputs to find potential security vulnerabilities or unexpected issues. While not replacements for hand-written tests, these augment the requirements-driven tests that you can write for your systems to find potential faults earlier in the development process.

- **Use as much production exposure as you can to test your system.** Testing in production at small scales (also known as Canary testing) lets you get the most real testing that your system can get. Incorporate testing in production as a key gate in your application delivery and deployment pipeline.

- **Leverage AI and LLMs to increase your testing coverage.** If you can get access to GitHub Copilot or similar technologies, consider using them (after consulting with legal counsel about the implications of this for your company and code) to fill out the unit, integration, and system tests for your existing systems. Or, if you're starting with TDD, consider AI automation for reducing the time to develop these tests in the inner loop. After all, if developer time spent on coding up tests is a concern, then AI should be a good way to reduce that cost.

As systems get more and more complex as they become distributed and handle ever larger scales, automated testing is only going to be more important to ensuring quality and correctness of the various interacting systems we're developing.

Conclusion

Writing and maintaining effective automated tests that represent the key requirements of a software system is becoming a sought after and important skillset for software engineering professionals today.

Gone are the days of having testing specialists just like how everyone is now a developer and an operations engineer.

Modern software engineering demands that every software engineering practitioner knows and understands the value of automated testing in how it affects the robustness, quality, and effectiveness of the software systems we're delivering to our customers.

At the end of the day, software engineering is about building the right thing to solve the right problem. Knowing what the requirements are to solving that problem is key to being able to solve it effectively.

Questions

Use these questions to reflect on your and your organisation's software testing practices:

- Do you have any automated tests? How hard would it be for you to start writing some for your solutions?

- Do you already follow TDD/BDD in your personal software engineering practice? Is your team already following it? Does your organisation? If not, have you examined the objections and reasons why? Have you found any bugs in production that you could have avoided by following TDD/BDD or at least having automated testing as part of the CI/CD process?

- If you are a decision maker in your organisation, what do you think would take to change the attitudes towards ensuring the quality of the solution sooner in the process than later? Will the insurance argument make sense — pay some amount of time now to avoid having to pay too much in the future? How about the investment argument for slower short-term returns but having longer-term benefits in quality? Will success stories and case studies be more convincing?

- Are your test only concerned with functional aspects of the system? Have you implemented quality or non-functional requirement tests?

- Do you use automated fuzzing solutions yet? Is this something your organisation will benefit from to find bugs before software reaches production and breaks due to well-crafted inputs?

- Does your culture prioritise testing as a practice? If not, have you examined why not?

Chapter 3: Documentation

"I have only made this letter longer because I have not had the time to make it shorter." – Blaise Pascal

Documentation is a perennially controversial topic because, in my experience, software engineering has focused so much on the business value of artefacts like the source code and shipping features more than others. I constantly hear folks saying that we should only be writing the documentation that's required in Agile practices, or that writing design documents is not a good use of time. There's some truth to these sayings and it's usually because the documentation being developed isn't providing lasting value to the audience it's meant to serve.

When I hear another software engineer complain about bad documentation that someone else wrote, I keep thinking about why we bother writing them at all. Sometimes though I come across very well-written documentation that I'm reminded why it's worth doing. Unfortunately, this points out something potentially obvious to a lot of people but may not be obvious to some: documentation is more an art than a science, and most software engineers aren't artists.

In fact, there are so many skills involved in writing effectively that it's just not innate to someone trained in logic and precision when telling a computer to do something. If I personally didn't learn about nor try to excel at writing, I can easily see myself in the camp of "read the code" to understand what it's doing and not bother with comments or any other forms of documentation. But I have, in my ~20-year career as a software engineer, found that the well-placed comment to explain why something is implemented a certain way, or a document describing the trade-offs made where other approaches were rejected, saved me so much time and bother in getting up to speed and making changes to the code base.

And there, friends, is where the value lies.

Good documentation keeps its audience in mind and provides a perspective to facilitate understanding.

Filling the gap

When I was at Friendster, I joined a software engineering group that had a lot of challenges cropping up from production constantly, and a fast-paced environment that aimed to deliver features while building upon key intellectual property that they held. See, at the time, Friendster had a <u>patent on something called the Graph Server</u> which is the core piece of technology that maintains the connections between users – or "friends".

The idea is, that you'd maintain an adjacency list and "shard" these across a number of Memcache server pools – you can configure the pools such that you can have a ring of N Memcache servers and a pool size of 3, you'd have a pool consisting of 3 logically adjacent servers where a copy of the data would reside. This brought in redundancy in case one of the memcache servers went down but also allowed the clients to pick 1 of the 3 to request data from on the read path and write to all 3 in the write path.

There were more advantages to this design, but that's not the point of this chapter.

This Graph Server was the component I worked on to improve its resilience, efficiency, performance, and scalability. We largely succeeded in that goal with the tools we had available to us in 2007–2008.

What we also didn't have at the time was good documentation to start with.

The Graph Server was implemented as a C++ service handling HTTP 1.0/1.1 requests, where the HTTP URIs indicated certain operations. This wasn't exactly a REST API, because it didn't allow mutation, and this was before resource-based API designs were popular. What the implementation didn't have was enough comments or documented design decisions on why it was implemented the way it was.

In Chapter 1, I described this to some degree, and in Chapter 2, I described how we initiated the project to write the replacement from scratch. In this chapter, I describe how we filled the documentation gap incrementally with different kinds of documentation.

Types of Documentation

There are many kinds of documentation – in fact, what you're reading right now is one kind of documentation (some might call this a Knowledge Base Article, but we'll talk about knowledge bases and how to build them another time). In this article, we're going to cover some that are relevant to typical software engineering projects. These are:

- **In-line/Code Documentation**: These are typically hosted within the program source code as comments which describe some aspect of the adjacent code. Sometimes these are parsed and extracted to be viewed as external artefacts like HTML or PDF files alongside program structure using automated tooling.

- **System Documentation**: These are typically standalone documents that depict the system (with or without diagrams) and the interacting components. In some places, these are called System Design Documents, Technical Design Documents, or Software Design Documents and follow a predefined template or at least cover system-level properties.

- **User Manuals**: These are user-facing documents for how a user can interact with a system, what the expected outcomes are, any error modes, and examples that illustrate canonical usage.

- **Operations Manuals**: These are operator-facing documents describing how a system should be operated (how it's configured, deployed, monitored, etc.) and how to troubleshoot the system when it's not operating as expected.

Some documentation that might fall outside of this set above could still be useful but is typically produced on an as-needed basis. These are things like **Architecture Decision Records** (to document trade-offs and decisions made), **Technical Proposals** (in some projects these are either documents or tickets in an engineering work tracking system), **User Stories** (specifications of functionality that are missing or meant to be supported), and **Defect Reports** or **Change Requests** (in some places where formal processes require documenting any deviations from previously agreed upon or delivered features). I won't be covering any of these but rest assured that these are valuable for the same reasons I'll be covering below.

Why write documentation?

This is always the unanswered question that a lot of people are afraid to ask, or have made their mind up on one way or another. I'm here to offer a perspective that might convince you that writing *effective* documentation is a goal worth pursuing.

1. **Why something is the way it is, is better explicit than inferred.** Explaining why a certain algorithm is used, or how the ordering of fields is important, or even why something is named the way it is along with what alternative names could have been used makes reading and understanding the system easier.

2. **In a team sport like software engineering, getting and staying on the same page lets the team work on the same goal collectively.** Nothing is worse than being on a team that doesn't understand the structure of the code, who steps on each others' work and doesn't maintain good lines of communication. When the person who has more time than sense just goes on and rewrites 60% of the code without first understanding what the goal was of the original structure, it saps the team's morale and makes a toxic team environment. Or does so and doesn't communicate why the change needed to be made. Being on the same page allows everyone to be included and aligned with what you're all working towards – this facilitates teamwork and collaboration more effectively.

3. **Documenting the problem, the available solutions and a plan to deliver value sets everyone up for success.** At the very least, doing so makes it clear what problem you and your team are trying to solve and what solutions are available – and which one you've picked – makes it clear to whoever is reading (the team, the stakeholders, management, the customer) how you intend to deliver value. If you cannot write this down and get the

stakeholders to agree, then you have your work cut out for you if you just dive into coding and hope it will all work out. *Hope is not a strategy.*

These are just a few reasons why writing documentation is important. I'm sure there are many more reasons that I've missed, but for the next section, I'm going to attempt to describe what effective documentation looks like given the reason I've laid out above.

What does effective documentation look like?

There are four key properties of effective documentation:

- Clarity
- Completeness
- Consistency
- Relevance / Being up-to-date

These should all be measured against the perspective of the intended audience of the documentation. As hinted at above, there are usually three main audiences for software engineering documentation:

- Users
- Software Engineers
- Operators

These audiences may be the same set of people (e.g., software tools targeting software engineers that also run the system themselves) but their concerns are well-defined and can be made independent of each other.

One tenet of effective writing I've learned over the years is: *Keep Your Audience in Mind.*

In the following sections, I'll cover each of the key properties and how you can tell whether your documentation is effective.

Clarity

When something is clear, it is unambiguous and does not leave room for misinterpretation.

Writing clearly requires having a singular focus and using words to convey that meaning without being distracting.

Avoid jargon where possible, and when jargon is being used, clarify its meaning by defining it once in a canonical location (like a glossary of terms).

Here are a few things I do to help ensure that the documentation I write is clear:

- **Test the documentation on the audience and solicit feedback on clarity.** You may think it's already clear, but unless you get feedback from the audience that it is clear, you don't really know.

- **Ask folks I trust to give a critique of the documentation aiming for maximum clarity.** It helps if this other person is not deeply familiar with the problem and/or solution space. This helps identify my biases and blind spots and helps me improve my documentation writing skills in the future.

- **Write different versions of the same sentence/paragraph and use the audience perspective to see which one might be clearer, before committing to one.** This is time-consuming but I've found has led to better quality outcomes in the past.

The goal of writing clearly is to reduce the friction for understanding.

Clearly written documentation is effective when folks reading the documentation end up with a good understanding of what the document is about and with less questions than they began with.

If your documentation is causing people to ask you questions even after they're read it, then your documentation isn't clear enough yet.

Completeness

Documentation is complete when it covers all the relevant parts of the solution from the intended audience's perspective.

Knowing the relevant parts based on the audience should not be hard, as long as you have open lines of communication with them. Imagining a customer is going to be hard, so talking to a real one is better. Or, only getting your perspective as a software engineer and assuming every other software engineer will have the same concerns as yours isn't likely to yield complete documentation.

This may be time-consuming and is where typically a lot of push-back comes through – software engineers do not typically excel in documentation writing because it's not seen as a problem-solving exercise. If however you do treat it like a problem that needs to be solved, most software engineers will find a way to either automate the process or solve it once and for all.

At Google, there's a high standard placed on the documentation of public interfaces. With hundreds and millions of lines of code I was very surprised at how good the function documentation was. Even better was when if something wasn't complete, someone treated that as an issue and would attempt to fix it sooner than later (no broken windows and all that goodness).

You know your documentation is complete when it answers some key questions from your audience's perspective:

- **What are the features of this solution?** If it's a function in code, what are the arguments, how does it affect the result, how does it fail, and what can it do? If it's a tool, what are the options/commands, how does it take the input, in what format, what is the output, etc.?

- **Where is further documentation if I need more information?** Say, from a command-line tool, there might be a `-help` option that has some information, but there could be a link to more comprehensive documentation. If the user manual doesn't cover every available option, then maybe some online documentation of options generated from in-line comments might be helpful to link.

- **How does the solution work?** Does it have dependencies that are needed in its operation? Are there features that only work with certain hardware/software packages? It may surprise you that even users want to know how a particular piece of software works even if they're not software engineers themselves, so for completeness, this information should be part of the documentation.

- **Who is the software intended for?** Documenting this explicitly counts towards completeness.

- **When should this software be used?** Another way of putting this is, what are the problems this software is intended to solve? If you know about situations where the software should not be used, citing those as examples explicitly will be helpful.

- **Why does this software exist?** This goes to trade-offs – was this built because something which already exists doesn't meet the requirements? What were those requirements (document them)?

This is probably where software engineers like me would look and say "too hard; is there an 80/20 solution to the problem?" And my answer would be yes – but knowing which 20% of documentation can yield the 80% value is harder than covering 100% of the concerns.

Note that *documentation doesn't have to be long to be complete*.

Consistency

Effective documentation will use the same words, style, and tone consistently throughout.

At Google, we had a style guide not just for covering the code but also the documentation for public interfaces. This helped greatly with reading and writing documentation because there was a consistent guideline that everyone would follow and hold each other accountable to. It's this community and cultural aspect that I cherished the most in my time there.

Even though there's room for originality and creativity (e.g., you can have user manuals that were humorous or playful) the approach to documentation was consistent – (e.g., every project needs a README.md). This consistency makes each cross-linked document searchable and therefore easily discoverable. If a project depends on another, then you can follow the documentation links or even the implementation to determine what the relation was.

Self-consistency is important for standalone documentation, like for design documents, so that a reader of the document doesn't have to be distracted by different words being used for the same thing. Using the same words across multiple documents reduces the likelihood of confusion for readers who have an understanding of related domains.

You know your documentation is consistent when readers don't complain about the confusion of the terms being used in your documentation.

Relevance / Being up-to-date

Nothing is worse than documentation that's out-of-date.

At best, the documentation is slightly wrong, and at worst it's actively misleading the reader. I've felt the need multiple times in my career to just go send a pull request to out-of-date documentation to just delete it. Thankfully the one time I did this myself, the project owners were thankful for it.

The value of documentation comes from being both accurate and relevant. When documentation is no longer describing the reality of the implementation, then it's no longer accurate nor relevant. Likewise, when the documentation is pointing towards a direction that is no longer where the project is going, then it's no longer accurate or relevant. In both cases, cultivating the documentation to remain accurate and relevant should be a part of the normal course of software engineering.

In our effort to rewrite the C++-based Graph Server, we ensured that every time we changed the implementation, we changed the documentation. We used Doxygen to generate the docs along with the UML relations, stashed those alongside the code, and kept them up-to-date. We had a Wiki where we defined the terms, the project goals, and the features we'd already delivered. Performance numbers were also in the Wiki. Production tests and the results were documented there as well.

If someone were to jump into the project, we made sure that the documentation was sufficient for them to get in there and be productive with their own ramp-up pace being the limiting factor. Of course, we would help them along but we relied heavily on the documentation to communicate between the Operations team, the product team, other members of the engineering team, and management.

At Google, I got to use a system that you can configure to automatically check the last update time of documentation hosted in the code base and file bugs to the team that owns the documentation for them to review and update appropriately. This made documentation management part of the maintenance of the system, which makes it something that's treated with respect.

Documentation that's stale and left so becomes an artefact of history. What we should want from the documentation is a reflection of reality.

Documentation in Open Source Projects

One key success story for documentation and its value to the community of software engineers and users is how Open Source projects live and die by the availability of effective documentation.

The quality of documentation for projects like Rust, Python, OCaml, Zig, C#, Java, and the LLVM compiler toolchain, for example, is exemplary of the kinds of documentation that yield value to the users and software engineers that work on the projects.

Projects in the Cloud Native Computing Foundation (CNCF) for instance have a documentation quality bar that they need to meet, and for good reason – these foundational pieces that power most modern software engineering projects require high quality documentation to reduce the maintenance and operational burden of new systems. Kubernetes, gRPC, and Istio for example have very well written documentation to allow developers to get up and running with modern system architectures.

Imagine not having access to the high quality documentation for these systems and having to learn them just from the code. I know I'd move on to a different industry if that would have been the working conditions I'd be asked to work under!

Despite the code being open and available, it's great foresight from these project maintainers and communities around them that value effective documentation enough to invest in it for the good of the audiences they serve.

Conclusion

Over my ~20-year career, I would be lying if I said I didn't enjoy writing documentation. I personally believe that writing effective documentation is a key skill that all software engineers should invest in, not just for the value it brings, but for how the skill translates into many aspects of software engineering.

Being able to write out ideas in a form that others can understand is the crux of what modern software engineering is all about.

The team sport of software engineering is only going to become more about collaborating, documenting, and problem-solving than actually writing code by hand. In fact, in modern software engineering, writing the code is not an important part anymore. It's the process of getting an idea written out, critiqued by colleagues, refined with a plan, then executing with top velocity with a shared goal in mind – that is where the value is.

When effective documentation is prioritised, we can see the positive outcomes in Open Source software.

There should be nothing stopping you and your team from doing modern software engineering by following the same model.

Questions

Use the following questions to reflect on how you, your team, or organisation treat software documentation:

- Are you investing in writing and maintaining software related documentation?

- Do you write and review design documents? How about software requirements?

- In your organisation, how is documentation treated? Is it valued the same as the software? Is it valued more? Have you investigated the reasons for over- or under-valuing documentation?

- What are the best examples of documentation you've seen out in the wild? What's stopping you from adopting their style for the documents you write?

- Do you get enough practice and feedback on writing documentation? Is this something you would like to get better in? Do you have mentors or peers who can give you pointers?

- Does your organisation have a style guide for documents? Do you have templates? Is there a standard for what constitutes good documents?

Chapter 4: Deployment

We keep moving forward, opening new doors, and doing new things, because we're curious and curiosity keeps leading us down new paths. — Walt Disney

Modern software, especially those that are deployed through the Internet, has gone through many iterations over the past couple of decades. Ever since ubiquitous internet access became commonplace and as more bandwidth became available to more people in the world, the cost of reaching potential customers has gone down significantly for most software providers. Today, even the Windows operating system has parts of it being deployed as a web application with back-ends powered by the cloud.

It was around the time of Internet Explorer and Netscape, and the explosion of Internet Protocol (IP) networks that are open to the public allowing practically anybody who can connect to an Internet Service Provider (ISP) and start participating in the open Internet, that software stopped just being something that came in a disc that was installed on your computer. Countless web-based applications started propping up, with Adobe Flash widgets, Java Applets, and the surviving technology that is JavaScript that's now as ubiquitous as the web browsers of the day. Now, instead of having just two web browsers, we have access to so many that it's a miracle that the web still works with all this diversity.

The modern approach to software combines the deployment of the "client" or "front-end" code either to a browser or to an application for a target platform (think mobile or desktop applications) and services that power these applications from afar, or "in the cloud". This architecture can be seen even for software that didn't typically follow this service-based deployment model — office productivity applications typically have a cloud component for collaborative editing support, or virtual drives that synchronise data across multiple computers, and even video games that have some multi-player component (even if it's just a global leaderboard).

With this modern architecture, the challenge of keeping the services up and running while enabling teams to iterate on any part of the system independently is an operational and execution challenge. It's taken us decades as an industry to just even have a shared expectation that our services must have the highest level of availability and resilience, and we're just catching up to the reality that we need better security practices for our customers' sakes.

In Chapter 1 I wrote about the properties of a well-designed modern software system, and in Chapter 2 I wrote about how to specify and test these systems. In Chapter 3 I wrote about how important documentation is for the engineering team and the users of the systems we build.

In this chapter, I dive into some of the intricacies of modern deployment techniques, especially for Software as a Service (SaaS) systems, which make up more and more of the modern software systems we develop today.

One step at a time

If releasing is hard, people will always find a reason not to release. — Gereon Hermkes

Previously I've described how we reimplemented a core service while I was at Friendster called the Graph Server. The challenge here was that this was 2007 and we were running bare metal machines to get the most out of the hardware we had in production. I remember first seeing the specs of the servers and being impressed with AMD Opteron CPUs that had multiple cores, and wondering what I could do with those! It turns out, we were able to serve ~5,000 queries per second for the friend lookups at 20% of the CPU per machine and we had 5 serving the bulk of the fast queries. The original implementation couldn't crack 1,200 queries per second at 60% CPU utilization and also required 100% of the RAM available on the machine (due to several memory leaks).

There was one key challenge for us though, and it came in the form of deployment — how do we safely deploy the memcache-backed graph servers without disruption to the live service?

Back then, we had dedicated load balancers that can do HTTP request multiplexing to defined back-ends. These load balancers were appliances that were tuned and dedicated to performing one function alone, and it was to present an HTTP interface on one IP address and make the requisite connections to the back-ends and load balance the requests. The PHP-based front-end servers would be connecting to the load balancers and making the requests to the graph server API.

The strategy we took, before we had a name for it, was to deploy the new version of the graph server and the accompanying memcache servers, set them up so that they're able to serve some live traffic, and then gradually introduce the graph servers into the pool of live servers known to the load balancer. It turns out this strategy is very similar to what's nowadays called "blue-green" deployments because we can then re-use the servers that had the old graph servers to host new versions of the code in the future and introduce them into the serving pool again.

I still remember the feeling I had when the ops team put some of the first few graph servers into the load balancer configuration. I had this sense of dread when the servers didn't immediately crash, and I panicked a little when we saw the CPU utilization of the first "fast" graph servers barely register any. What we also noticed was that the front-end servers hitting the new graph servers had lower latencies, but we're still serving HTTP 200 responses to users. Everything seemed to be pointing toward the new version of the graph server at 5% traffic was holding up!

The decision was made to increase the percentage gradually, and as we reached 100% of traffic being routed to the new version of the graph server, it was mission accomplished. This process allowed us to reduce the overall footprint of the graph server by 50% with enough headroom to grow another 3x.

What allowed the team to deliver the change successfully and safely was threefold:

- **We had an amazing set of people who put processes in place to mitigate the risk of bugs causing issues in production.** There were no corners cut during the code reviews, no shortcuts taken when deploying new versions of code, and for large changes, we made sure we had contingency plans and had ways to back out in an orderly manner if we needed to.

- **The infrastructure in place allowed us to make gradual and deliberate deployment decisions.** Having the load balancers, configuration, and monitoring in place allowed us to determine with high confidence that the changes we were making were working as intended.

- **We made building and deploying new versions of the graph server easier, so frequent releases could be made going forward.** The previous version of the graph server needed a lot of initialisation time and had very little in the way of configuration options. The new version allowed us to configure features with flags so that we can turn on/off features independent of the version deployed in production.

Because it was now easier to build and deploy the graph server, improvements we made over time got deployed more quickly and as safely as when we did so the first time. This story would have turned out very differently if we didn't prioritise and internalise the importance of following a good deployment model during the development process. It also would have turned out badly if we didn't take care we did in ensuring that major changes are treated as special.

Now, as you may already know, Friendster is no longer in operation, and I can tell the story of the technical failings we had that ultimately caused it to lose users to Facebook, but that's for another day.

For now, let's look into modern software engineering practices when it comes to deployment models and strategies.

Deployment Models

There are three typical deployment models for SaaS solutions:

- **On-Premises**: where the service provider owns and operates hardware that they maintain, either in facilities (i.e., a datacenter) that they own or lease.

- **Cloud**: where the service provider outsources the infrastructure or platform upon which the software is deployed, typically on a pay-per-use or pay-per-resource basis. Typically, these clouds are available to the public as well, where there are multiple other tenants that would be running their software on the same hardware owned by the cloud provider.

- **Hybrid**: where the service provider hosts part of the service they provide in both on-premise hardware and via cloud providers. This is popular for performing data warehousing and analytics functionality where sensitive transactional data and processing happens on-premises while everything else happens in the cloud. Some organisations tend to leverage existing hardware investments and use the cloud for burst or out-of-band operational purposes.

Which model works best depends on the requirements of the SaaS solution.

It's worth noting that, depending on the scale of the operation, on-premises solutions might become more cost effective especially if the operational costs of hosting in the cloud start eroding the margins for the business.

There are many stories out there of companies choosing to move from the cloud to on-premise solutions for a better return on investment — if this is something you're contemplating, consider the operational burden of actually running your own machines and the insurance cost of having redundant sites for disaster recovery.

One thing that's important to consider is the "unit economics" of the SaaS solution — consider the cost of providing the service on a "per-unit" basis, whether that's an API request, storage volume, or unit of value being provided by the solution. If staying in the cloud and scaling on demand still allows you to maintain the unit economics and margin for your business, then the flexibility of the cloud might be best for your use case. Otherwise, opting for a hybrid model might allow you to only use the cloud footprint for burst capacity and pay for what you use and only in overload situations while leveraging your existing hardware investments and capital expenditure.

If you're a decision maker for your organisation, work with your finance professional and/or a competent technology professional for making the Total Cost of Ownership calculations on whether on-premises, cloud, or hybrid deployments are the best for your organisation.

Deployment Strategies

Once you know your deployment model, let's discuss some of the available deployment strategies for SaaS solutions:

- Blue-Green Deployments
- Canary Rollouts
- Rolling Updates

Blue-Green Deployments

As I described earlier, Blue-Green Deployments typically involve setting up infrastructure labeled "blue" and "green". For example, you might label some nodes in Kubernetes with "blue" and "green", and when deploying new pods have the new version be deployed to the "green" nodes where testing can commence, and traffic can be routed gradually to the new pods in the "green" nodes. Once all traffic has been routed to the new pods, the pods in the "blue" nodes can be turned down.

This strategy is good for the following reasons:

- **It makes rollbacks easy.** Because the old version of the services are still running on the "blue" nodes, traffic can be routed back to them easily.

- **It makes debugging easy.** Because the green environment will generate logs and telemetry, having it isolated from the previous version lets you better see the differences.

- **It allows groups of services to be deployed and tested together.** You can extend this model to not just a single service but a set of services that must be released together as a group.

The largest reason for not always using blue-green deployments is the fact that this can easily double the required footprint for deployments. It's plausible as a strategy to use when there's a fairly large risk that a change might require a quick roll-back, or that a change being deployed is complex enough that it requires additional testing.

Either way, consider the cost of doing blue-green deployments against the benefits that you gain from it.

Canary Rollouts

Have you ever heard the phrase "the canary in the coal mine"?

The idea was to bring a canary (a small bird in a cage) down to the mine. Canaries are typically chirpy birds so they make a lot of noise when they're in a cage. If the mine experiences a sudden drop in available oxygen or an increase in toxic gasses, the little chirpy bird is usually the first one to faint and stop making noises — thus it was (morbid and inhumane as it is) an early warning mechanism for miners to get out as soon as they can.

Canary rollouts follow the same strategy but in software — a new version of a service is deployed in production taking a small percentage of traffic to see whether things went as planned. This assumes that you have enough replicas of a service where a new version of the service can be deployed first with a few instances, then growing to eventually replace all the replicas with the new version.

This strategy is good for the following reasons:

- It allows direct exposure of new versions of code to production.

- It allows exposing configuration changes to production in a limited fashion, not just new versions of code to production.

- It facilitates an experimental approach to deploying new features and services.

Key to having a successful canary deployment/rollout is having sufficient telemetry and system observability to determine whether the new version of code or a configuration change will cause measurable disruption in production. This only works if you can tell whether a 1% traffic test produces enough signals to determine the relative safety of a change.

The largest downside to this approach is the need to monitor key metrics that you may or may not already have defined for the service. While it's useful to rely on some default metrics like error rates and resource utilisation, there's no substitute for Service Level Indicators (SLIs) and Service Level Objectives (SLOs).

Another downside is the relative complexity of gradually introducing changes as your multi-service architecture gets more complex. Compared to Blue-Green Deployments, Canary rollouts rely on the idea of in-place replacements and gradual traffic re-routing, something that can be easy to get wrong and may rely on some manual actions to accomplish.

Rolling Updates

Perhaps the simplest approach for deploying changes to production is by performing updates in a rolling fashion, updating replicas of a service gradually until all replicas have the same version and configuration. This approach ensures that changes are made to minimise the amount of downtime for a service, and where possible, it can be configured to start conservatively and follow a growth function (successive doubling, power-law function, exponential scaling, fixed percentage change, etc.).

When coupled with monitoring and automation, rolling updates can be set-up to automatically roll back if a change causes disruption (similar to canary rollouts) or accelerate change if the monitoring indicates that good things are happening.

The key downside to rolling updates is that it typically only affects a single service's deployment. If you're deploying a set of services together or updating them together, rolling updates can get complicated especially if you need to have complex routing rules for inter-service communication. In these situations, you might be better suited by blue-green deployments or even canary rollouts of new code versions and using rolling updates for enabling/disabling feature flags.

Tooling

So far we've been looking at deployment models and strategies, but it's important that in this modern software engineering landscape we understand the available tooling and technologies that make these approaches possible.

Automation in Deployment

The key to a successful deployment story nowadays is in leveraging automation tools and services as much as you can. Whether you're deploying services on-premises, in the cloud, or in a hybrid environment, you must use the available automation tools to codify and embed the complexity of the deployment in configuration (treating it like code).

There are key areas of automation where the most leverage can be had:

- **Continuous Integration (CI) / Continuous Delivery (CD)**: ensuring that not only is testing continuous in your CI solution, but that deployment is part of the day-to-day operations through CD.

- **Infrastructure as Code (IaC)**: ensuring that infrastructure setup is repeatable, auditable, and automated gives developers the leverage to define the infrastructure once, maintain it as the architecture changes, and keep production in-sync with intent.

- **GitOps**: using Software Configuration Management (SCM) tooling to drive IaC and CD, where there's a central definition of the intended state of the system and the deployment actions are performed to meet that state. It's control theory and control systems meeting SCM and CI/CD. In this case, the SCM of choice is Git.

The goal in modern software engineering is to make deployment a matter of making changes to committed configuration and be driven by changes to code and associated artefacts instead of manual actions as much as possible.

Containerisation and Orchestration

No discussion of modern software engineering deployment is complete without the mention of application containerisation and container orchestration and the most popular solutions in this area: Docker and Kubernetes. Certainly, if you're starting a SaaS solution today whether you're deploying on-premise, in the cloud, or in a hybrid environment, it would be prudent to build around containers and a container orchestrator.

Docker allows developers to define a self-contained deployable artefact (a container image) which can then be picked up and deployed across a set of nodes managed by Kubernetes. This changes not just the deployment mechanism but also the way software is built and tested. If you're able to build a Docker container with your code in it, it most certainly can be run and tested within that container. The same tested container image can then be deployed on a Kubernetes cluster to serve test or production traffic.

All the deployment strategies we discussed above can be implemented by automation and tooling that builds upon the Kubernetes orchestration model. My favourite projects that facilitate automation and service routing are ArgoCD, Istio, Prometheus, and OpenTelemetry.

Conclusion

I bring concepts touched upon in the first three chapters where I discuss how modern software solutions that are distributed and service-oriented are deployed to reduce downtime and manage risk by deploying changes more often as part of the development pipeline.

I also note that automation is a key aspect of modern software engineering, so much so that infrastructure, configuration, and deployments are treated and managed as code.

Finally, I point out the shift in software development with the advent of containers and container orchestration systems, making the deployment story more uniform and operationally consistent than it's ever been.

With SaaS systems, it becomes both easier to deploy changes to production, but with this ease comes sophistication to increase confidence that new versions of the code do not break user experiences.

Questions

If you are working on SaaS systems, consider the following questions to reflect upon your deployment practices:

- Do you have deployment automation set up for your solution?

- How long do your deployments take and how costly are mistakes for your software? Have you considered investing in making deployment more automatic and less expensive? Have you thought about how to mitigate the cost of mistakes through your deployment practices?

- Are you doing manual deployments of your solutions? How do you ensure that the updates are not breaking customers/users?

- If there were any changes you needed to make to your infrastructure, are you able to make them automatically? Do you use technologies that allow you to refer to a source of truth for the desired state of your production system?

- How are configuration changes deployed to production? Are you following Safe Deployment Practices?

- If you are a decision maker in your organisation, are you aware of how costly your deployment processes are? Do you know how long it takes for a change to make it to production? Do you know how confident the team is in getting changes safely into production?

- Does your team have a culture of fear around deploying changes to production? Have you thought about how to address this fear?

Chapter 5: Continuous Evolution

"If you don't evolve, you will die. "— Marcus Lemonis

This is the final chapter of this volume on Modern Software Engineering. The first four chapters cover Systems Design, Testing, Documentation, and Deployment.

In this chapter, I'm going into how these four previous parts contribute to a modern approach to software engineering which has proven itself over the past two decades of innovation — going from shrink-wrapped software distributed in physical media installed on personal or shared computers to software as a service accessed through web browsers or thin client applications and hosted in the cloud.

I'm also going beyond this to glimpse a possible future that's shaping up to be a potential disruption to the whole software industry with the rise of AI assistants and generative AI.

Cautionary Tale

In November 2008, Friendster suffered a prolonged outage when a power outage in the datacenter where all of the infrastructure was hosted (a single point of failure) took it down. This meant all the application servers, load balancers, database servers, and caches — literally all the machines running Friendster — were down.

I mentioned that memcached servers had backed the Graph Server I was working on to keep the friends lists for everyone quickly accessible and served when required. Unfortunately, re-hydrating this cache from nothing was done with a single-threaded application that queried the database and placed the data into the cache one user at a time. This isn't the most efficient way to do it, but before this outage, we never had the need to speed this up.

The other part of this story was that I had already written a multi-machine and multi-threaded version of that tool, but it was stuck in code review for months. It was deemed low priority since we didn't foresee needing to bring up the graph server caches from scratch. We focused on the day-to-day and week-to-week enhancements needed to the service to optimise the latency, improve the logging, experiment with new approaches to computing "closeness," and leverage the data from the graph to help improve the product.

Murphy's law struck — anything that can go wrong will go wrong. And that one weekend in November 2008, the worst that could happen happened — we needed to bring up the graph server caches from scratch, and we only had the old way of doing it that couldn't handle the scale we had grown to while the replacement has not been tested nor code reviewed. Then, under pressure not just from business continuity concerns but also from competitor pressure (at that time, Facebook was just starting to grow into the markets where Friendster was still popular), every hour we weren't serving the site meant we became less relevant, so we committed two cardinal Engineering sins:

- Built C++ applications without "-Wall."

- Ran an untested solution direct to production.

The first one was directly my fault — I had set up the build files but forgot to add the "warn on all potential issues" flag in the build. Because the Graph Server represented each user's ID as a 64-bit integer, the code I wrote had not explicitly used int64 to represent the user ids, which defaults to 32-bit integers. This meant that some user ids had been truncated to 32 bits, and since we never reused user ids, the numbers got converted silently without the compiler warning. The application happily completed quickly, cutting down the recovery time from an estimated 24H down to half an hour using many machines to rehydrate the cache. Except it was rehydrating the cache with the wrong data very quickly.

It's no good being fast when you're wrong.

The second part is where we thought the rehydration had been completed successfully but then learned from users that their friends' lists had been incomplete and/or had people on there that they didn't know. Because we ran untested code direct to production in a situation where the stakes were very high, we learned quickly that losing users' trust is the best way to give them a reason to leave you for your competitors. I reckon Facebook grew a few million active users during that Friendster outage, and ever since then, Friendster would not recover.

I left Friendster in June 2009, and while it kept operating for a few more years, the investors and new owners eventually made the (good) call in 2010 to sell the patents covering the Graph Server to Facebook.

This experience I had early in my career taught me the lessons of what both good engineering practices look like and what the consequences of bad engineering practices could be — it can quite literally fail spectacularly to a point where it can bring down a whole company. This is why I try my best to share the stories and lessons I've learned going through this journey so that we get better engineering outcomes for society.

Friendster did evolve, but it didn't evolve fast enough to address key risks like not diversifying its deployment footprint, not having tested a disaster recovery plan, and not evolving the product to meet the challenges of the competition.

What can we learn from this story of slow evolution, and how do modern software engineering practices address these concerns?

Agile and DevOps

I have a love-hate relationship with Agile development practices because it tends to be too rigid about what you should and shouldn't do — which is quite ironic given that it's supposed to be "agile." However, I see the benefits of a predictable engineering process that allows for priority-driven decision making and promotes the idea of building software to accommodate change.

However, I've found many cases where teams following the agile methodologies (whichever you chose) tend to forget what good design and good architecture look like, all in the service of hitting the sprint goals or maintaining the velocity measured in story points.

It can get absurd because folks that ascribe very heavily to the agile methodologies typically eschew documentation with the reasoning that "only produce the documentation you need" is good enough — until it isn't, because the code devolves into inconsistency and chaos.

I listened recently to a very good podcast from Software Engineering Radio (episode 574) which covers [Software as an Engineering Discipline](#) — I highly recommend giving this a listen if you want to hear some contrarian thoughts on the whole agile methodology practices that go against "design up front" practices.

My thoughts on this, having seen it in action in many places I've been, are as follows:

- **Agile methodologies are great for tracking implementation efforts and stakeholder management.** Having seen other ways of tracking implementation efforts with traditional project management approaches that work for construction and other physical projects, they tend to not work well for software systems because of their ephemeral and ultimately malleable form. Agile methodologies espouse continuous conversations and feedback gathering amongst the stakeholders (folks that need the product, those that are funding the effort, and those building the product) to ensure that what's being worked on is progressing and is the thing that should be built works well.

- **Agile methodologies offer tools for ensuring that priorities are in place and the requirements are being met.** Having a common vocabulary and shared understanding of what the priorities and requirements are lets the engineering team focus on the important features of a solution along with the constraints within which they would be working with. This vocabulary and shared understanding is key whether or not you follow agile processes, but the agile approaches do focus on clarifying these using techniques and practices that bring this to the forefront of the software engineering process.

- **Agile methodologies aren't great replacements for thoughtful design and architecture of sufficiently complex systems.** I've seen this fail so often that I'm not convinced that the few cases where this would have succeeded were because the engineering team had the required experience and discipline to build in design and architecture along the way. Just relying on continuous refactoring and eventually getting to a good design rarely works for sufficiently complex systems (e.g., compilers, databases, distributed systems that need strong consistency, etc.).

- **Agile approaches seem better than the rigid non-iterative approaches especially for continuously evolving products and services.** I've had my fair experience with non-Agile methodologies, and it's always a pain to have either requirements change in the middle of an effort or get to the end and get a product that no longer meets the new business realities. I personally wouldn't go back to that, although I'm partial to having the initial consultations be requirements-gathering exercises that can feed into an agile implementation approach.

- **Agile processes combined with thoughtful design and architecture practices yield more manageable software systems that can handle changes in requirements and priorities.** The most successful agile projects I've seen executed involve thoughtful up-front requirements gathering and thoughtful high-level design, which constantly evolve as the team learns new things while implementing the solutions. The iterative process applied to the design and implementation process has yielded the most successful products and solutions thus far, in my experience.

I don't think there's anything inherently wrong with the Agile methodologies — rather, they're a superior approach to running a software project compared to many of the other non-iterative approaches out there. However, I still believe the design process needs to also be prioritised especially for continuously evolving systems.

DevOps is another approach that tries to incorporate two parts of the engineering process into one — development and operations. It's a good idea at the surface: the team developing the solution should also be operating it. This makes the assumption, though, that software engineers know how to operate services in a production environment or that their learning how to do this will suddenly make the service better.

Like with Agile methodologies, I have a love-hate relationship with DevOps: when done well, you get good outcomes; when done wrong, you get catastrophic outcomes. The downsides are just too large compared to the upside, which is why folks are now learning that Platform Engineering is the discipline that empowers software engineering, especially for cloud-hosted services.

To be fair, I do think there are good things that come with following the DevOps model, even if and especially if you have a Platform Engineering function in your organisation:

- **Complete responsibility from development to production.** This empowers the engineering team to incorporate the production environment's needs into the development of the solution.

- **Empowerment to build or apply automation.** When the software engineers are responsible for deploying and running a service, they are also responsible for reducing the system's toil. They can lean on more automation and tooling than manual efforts. There should no longer be any excuse that the development team doesn't control the deployment process or the environment.

- **End-to-end visibility of the product's operational requirements.** Because it's now the software engineer's responsibility to ensure that the service works well in production, they are now also in the position to add the requisite observability signals to allow them to make data-driven decisions on the design and implementation of the system.

The parts I don't like about DevOps are the following:

- **Forcing software engineers to handle infrastructure.** It takes a completely different set of skills and expertise to operate and manage infrastructure, and asking software engineers to do it means it's a cost to their focus and productivity. It's a good idea to reach for, though, a software engineer should ideally understand the underlying infrastructure so that they can make better decisions on how to leverage them, but their time deciding whether to upgrade the underlying OS or use a more efficient machine is time taken away from making the solution better or making features that make the product more valuable.

- **Force-converting operations engineers to be software engineers.** The other direction also isn't ideal because the set of skills required to develop good quality software are completely different from executing safe rollouts of infrastructure or ensuring capacity is sufficient to handle growth. There's good reasons to have system administration and operations engineering skills because they're valuable in their own right, and forcing folks to also be software engineers means they don't get to use the expertise they've built up and try to evolve into a hybrid role.

- **Having a team of N doing DevOps means you have on average N/2 developer time and N/2 operations time.** This means you have no full-time software engineers to focus on software engineering and no full-time operations engineers to focus on the operations engineering. As N grows, your opportunity cost for either operations or software engineering grows. At a large enough N, it might make more sense to have dedicated operations and software engineering folks, in which case you're reaching the upper limits of when DevOps becomes sustainable.

DevOps does make sense for small teams working on small services and is a good start for setting up good practices and automation around building and deploying services. At some point, though, an organisation with enough DevOps teams will have to consider consolidating the platform-building and operations to a platforms engineering team to empower the DevOps teams to be more productive and scale to the demand of the organisation.

Continuous Integration, Delivery, and Deployment

In Chapter 4, I mentioned the many ways of deploying services in the context of Software as a Service systems. What we need to keep in context is that deployment is the tail end of the continuous evolution cycle and that the combination of Continuous Integration (CI), Continuous Delivery (CD), and Continuous Deployment (also CD) requires a coordinated effort to bake in automation into the engineering processes in the modern age.

Today, the typical SaaS deployment follows a process like the following:

1. A change is made to the source code, which triggers a build typically hosted in a container image.

2. This container image is then tested with automated test suites to verify whether the requirements are being met.

3. The successfully tested container image is then deployed to a test environment, typically mimicking the production environment with some test traffic going to this environment.

4. When this successfully qualified container image is marked for deployment, it is deployed gradually to production.

5. While the change is rolling out to production, it is monitored to determine whether the system works as expected. If the build progresses to replace all instances in production, the build is tagged as the "last known good." If it's rolled back because it was considered bad, then the "last known good" version is rolled in, and the build is marked bad.

6. Go back to 1.

You can then imagine this process happening on different schedules for different parts of the system, and the modern software engineering process accounts for that and prioritises continuous evolution and shortening the distance between a code change being made to that change being rolled out to users and customers. This process aims to empower the software engineering teams to set up the appropriate testing to catch issues earlier in the process.

This process also incentivises teams working on well-defined interface boundaries to reduce churn and apply an evolutionary approach to changing APIs and Data Contracts.

Version Control Systems

Modern software engineering requires tracking different software versions and allowing for collaborative development in a scalable fashion. The evolution of tools around Software Configuration Management (the other term for Version Control Systems) is fascinating, going back to the 1950s with physical media and manual processes to now being able to version container images.

The key thing, however, for using a version control system for source code is to enable navigating a project's history effectively to support operations like full or partial rollbacks of code changes and supporting multiple concurrent branches of development. A system that effectively tracks changes and manages the combination of these changes to support building a single solution or a related set of solutions is key to scalable software engineering on a single codebase.

Tools like Git and Mercurial allow large teams to collaborate in a distributed manner on the same codebase by supporting the sharing and synchronisation of a consistent history across multiple copies of the repository. The key data structure used in both Git and Mercurial is the [Merkle Tree](), which defines cryptographically strong provenance chains of changes, allowing users to determine whether the commit history has been tampered with. I highly recommend learning more about this data structure, even if only for your enjoyment.

On a more practical matter, having a source repository like a Git repository allows for both distributed development (each engineer will have a copy of the repository on their workstation) as well as coordinated and collaborative change integration (engineers send pull requests that can be merged into the main development line, usually with a code review process in place to ensure consistent quality and peer review of the implementation). A canonical repository can then be used to feed into a CI/CD system which automates the process of delivering the solution to production.

This concept can also be applied to managing the configuration of infrastructure and platforms (Infrastructure as Code or IaC) and driving the infrastructure configuration and deployment configuration from a Git repository. This is also referred to as the GitOps model, where the canonical or ideal state of the system is defined in a Git repository which is then automatically applied by automation agents to the infrastructure hosting the services.

As an aside, Generative AI solutions like ChatGPT and GitHub's Copilot can work with existing Git repositories to "learn" about what's in a codebase and provide suggestions to the developers as a virtual coding partner. Having used these tools extensively in my day-to-day work and in my personal projects, I'm convinced we'll end up solving more interesting problems with the help of these AI solutions. The trick is having enough infrastructure to leverage what these Generative AI solutions bring to the table to help fuel the system's continuous evolution.

Monitoring and Observability

The final and probably most important part of modern software engineering is the concept of Observability and how it's changed the way folks debug issues in production, identified optimisation opportunities, drove business decisions on areas of investment, and reduced engineering toil due to frequent interrupts.

If you haven't yet, I highly recommend picking up a copy of <u>Observability Engineering</u> which covers the history of how folks have handled the problem of debugging systems in production more completely. However, just briefly, there are three pillars to the Observability of software systems:

- **Logs** — these are either structured or unstructured timestamped data emitted by the application, which usually includes internal states and operations to look back at what the system was doing at a given time.

- **Metrics** — these are measurements with certain dimensions that represent interesting events, typically defined by the engineers to signify some core part of what the system is doing. These are typically counters of the number of times certain things occurred or certain amounts of resources consumed (CPU counters, Memory counters, etc.).

- **Traces** — these are timestamped and nested spans of operations that represent what the system was doing with additional semantic information. A particularly useful flavour of traces is distributed traces, where an operation that spans multiple machines/services can be traced and treated as a single operation through the same trace identifier.

What modern observability practices centre around is the combination of Logs, Metrics, and Traces to derive higher-level measures called System Level Indicators (SLIs) and Service Level Objectives (SLOs), which then also define an error budget for your service. I can't do the topic of SLIs/SLOs and error budgets justice in this article, but the [Google SRE books](#) also cover these in great detail.

One way to think about the role of Monitoring and Observability in Modern Software Engineering is to consider it as the data sources that allow you to experiment with new versions of software and system configurations to determine whether a change you're making is good or bad. Without monitoring and observability, you're not doing effective engineering nor following a scientific method of deciding whether a change you're making to the system is effective or significant.

Some recent developments in AI enable engineers to determine these indicators and metrics that correlate to outages and/or changes to the system. This AI-assisted approach is termed AIOps, where a lot of the previously manual definitions of metrics and alerts can be driven by AI models trained on the data produced by the system. This becomes more relevant as more complex interconnected systems with independently evolving parts start experiencing issues while humans haven't explicitly set up the alerting infrastructure through sheer complexity. AI assistance in this field can identify the easily-fixed issues and hidden correlations that would take humans deliberate effort and exploration to find.

At the heart of continuous evolution is an understanding that what you don't measure, you don't manage, so if you want to manage service quality, you start by measuring it. Only then can continuous evolution be guided by the data you're gathering.

Conclusion

Modern Software Engineering is all about the iterative process of identifying the requirements on the software, crafting a solution that's well tested and meets the requirements, deploying in a controlled but continuous manner, and finding ways to improve the practice from a personal level up to a full organisation.

The Engineering part of Software Engineering does not just apply to the process but to the mentality — using solid foundations and applying practical solutions to problems using software. In the Engineering process, there's planning, execution, and evaluation — things that we all should be doing in the practice of Software Engineering. The modern way of doing so is more iterative and data-driven.

Questions

Use the following to reflect upon your organisation's continuous evolution practices:

- Are we constantly evaluating how we are doing Software Engineering and improving it to deliver better software that's more secure, more performant, more efficient, and more maintainable?

- Is the organisation set up so that it can change the practices that aren't working? Or is it too tied to specific processes regardless of whether they work?

- At a personal level, are you continuously evolving? Do you have opportunities to learn new approaches? Do you have mentors, peers, or a network that you can learn from?

- Does your team or organisation have a continuous learning and improvement culture? If you're a decision maker, what would it take for you to consider instilling a culture of continuous learning and continuous improvement?

- Is your team or organisation learning from outages and consistently evaluating the effectiveness of your engineering process?

Epilogue

Thank you for reading this far in!

If you purchased this book from www.deanberris.com I'm grateful for your support. Thank you for trusting the value of the knowledge and experiences I've picked up along the way in my 20-year software engineering career.

If you found the questions intriguing and would like to talk about your personal, team, or organisational practices and gain an outsider's perspective on different things you can try, you can reach out to me@deanberris.com or book a consultation with me through the website (www.deanberris.com).

I'm happy to hear from you on which part of the book was most valuable to you.

If you were given a copy of this book, thank you for reading through all the way!

Please feel free to forward to friends and your peers.

At the time of this writing, I'm based in Sydney, New South Wales, Australia.

I'm looking forward to hearing from you!

Cheers,- Dean

www.ingramcontent.com/pod-product-compliance
Lightning Source LLC
Chambersburg PA
CBHW071109240526
45469CB00006BD/2408